A Place Called There

Evelyn Weber

WestBow
PRESS
A DIVISION OF THOMAS NELSON

WestBow Press books may be ordered through booksellers or by contacting:

WestBow Press
A Division of Thomas Nelson
1663 Liberty Drive
Bloomington, IN 47403
www.westbowpress.com
1-(866) 928-1240

Used King James Version, New International version, and Amplified Bible..

ISBN: 978-1-4497-0805-4 (sc)
ISBN: 978-1-4497-0846-7 (dj)
ISBN: 978-1-4497-0806-1 (e)

Library of Congress Control Number: 2010939773

Editor: Rocket Barber
Cover Artist : George Benetiz

Printed in the United States of America

WestBow Press rev. date: 3/8/2011

Foreword

WALKING WITH GOD AND ENJOYING the intimacy of serving Him often means walking close to the fire and feeling the heat.

Although believers and those close to the Lord have a covering, they are not always precluded from the pain and suffering that comes from living in a fallen world.

Because of the sacrifice that was made on the cross at Calvary, we are able to enter into a place of safety and security, which only comes with having an intimate relationship with our heavenly father.

As blood-washed children of God, we have access to the secret place of His presence. Here, we are welcome at any time and are able to abide under the shadow of the Almighty.

It is a place in the Spirit; "a place called there."

When you first meet Evelyn Weber, the first thing you notice is that she is full of exuberance and just oozes the joy of the Lord. It is as if her life has always been filled with happiness.

Later, when you get to know her a little better and she shares some of her past, you get an understanding that life has not always been easy for her and her family.

One wonders how she was able to survive the early years. Survival must have come at a price, as the paths of our spiritual journeys are often strewn with hurts. Her heart must have been stained with the pain of the past, yet she was able to come through in victory.

As a pastor and as a mother, she has known loss, yet she has been able to rise above her circumstances and press toward the prize of the higher calling that comes with spending time in a place called *there*.

Evelyn knows that this is her refuge, her fortress, and her home.

We know that as you read her story, your heart will be touched, and you will begin to understand that this place she visits is not a destination; it is a place that each and every one of us has access to in the Spirit; a place where we can find shelter from life's troubled storms.

We are blessed to count Evelyn and her family as our friends.

Evangelists David and June Thom
World Wide Evangelism RSA

Dedication

To my heavenly Father who dances on the wind,
to my Savior who draws me there,
And to the Holy Spirit who catches us when we
fall into eternity:
"My soul longs and pants after Thee."

To Higher Ground Ministries in Connecticut.
On my day of sorrow, you sang these words to
me:
"I need you."
"I need you, too, Beloved."

To my husband—my lover and best friend:
"Forever and then some."

To my children,
Christine, Nicholas, Dasha,
and, of course, Vincent,
aka "Vinny Bag of Doughnuts":
"Spaghetti for supper."

And the Lord said to Moses I will do this thing that you ask for you have found favor, loving mercy and kindness in my sight and I know you personally by name. And Moses said, show me your Glory. And God said I will make my goodness pass before you; for I will be gracious to whom I will be gracious; and will show mercy and loving kindness. But he said you cannot see my face for no man shall see me and live. And he said there is a place beside me, and there I shall take you and place you beside me, and you shall stand upon the rock, and while my Glory passes by, then I will take away my hand and you shall see my back; but my face shall not be seen.

Exodus 33:17–23

Prologue

OFTEN WHEN WE PLAN A journey, such as a vacation, we will read and study road maps to become familiar with our route, load our car, hook up a navigation system unit to our car, and follow the directions given to us by a woman whose recorded voice is calm, kind, and sure. After hours of driving, we will arrive and exclaim, "We're finally there!" The trip will be easy and seemingly routine.

Personal journeys are quite different. We plead with God to take us to a new place, a place where we imagine we will find complete wholeness and a sense of satisfaction that can only be experienced, indescribable with words. We fancy a destination we cannot explain, even with our most eloquent language. We begin our journey, following road signs along a path that will lead us through a *suffering place*. When we realize where we are heading, we must make a choice. Will we continue down the path and trust? Or will we allow instincts—our "fight or flight" response—to send us running?

When we reach the suffering place, we often find that we will sacrifice the nearest and dearest treasures that we hold closest to our hearts.

I want to share my journey with you. Some of you who read my story may one day travel a similar path, passing though a suffering place that makes you a member in a club you never wished to join. You will need the comfort of familiarity that comes from knowing you are not alone. Others, I hope, will know after reading this book that they are necessary and crucial elements in another person's healing process, even if their task is just to be there. Even if they have nothing to say, they can just be there.

On May 8, 2009, I reached my suffering place, and I thought the sacrifice I saw upon the altar there was the worst thing my eyes would ever behold; I drew closer and realized it was more difficult than I had imagined. What I thought was a loss was my own reflection. I was to be the sacrifice.

My journey begins in Good Samaritan Hospital, Long Island, New York. Or, perhaps, it begins just a bit before.

Contents

Chapter 1

December 3, 1980

I NEVER EXPECTED TO BE pregnant again. I had planned to have three children; no more. This, my fourth pregnancy, was an absolute shock. For four months, I was unable to be excited about the situation, but as I began my second trimester, I fell absolutely in love with the little gift inside me.

Finally, because I was thirty, I decided I was more mature than I had been with my earlier "planned" pregnancies. As a younger woman, I had worked so very hard, keeping a job while also attending nursing school, and I had missed my children so much. With this child, I decided I was more equipped to be the proverbial "perfect mom," and I even decided to use cloth diapers as an extension of this idea.

I knew as he was being born that this kid was different. I remember telling the nurses and doctor that he didn't want to be born. He grabbed hold of my legs as if to say, "I don't want to be out!" They had to pry his little hands loose! I appreciated the chance to hold my son in my arms in a way I could not have as a younger mother .Our lives were so hard it was just enough to think about where the next meal will come from, and do we have a safe place to live, I treasured every moment with my little boy as if this would make up for the loss of time with my other children. I guess you might say that I thought I could relive thorough my son what I could not do through his brothers and sister. I loved my children so much that I wanted to gain back the time lost the precious time that was taken from being a parent who alone had the awesome responsibility to raise her children. I realize now many years later that our heavenly father was so wise to say that it takes two to raise a child .He never meant for there to be single mothers due to divorce. So you can imagine how excited I was when the Dr. told me I was pregnant again. I remember thinking that he was so funny, this baby of mine, —even then. I never let a day go by without telling him how much I loved him. Not one.

I held my son and dreamed of a day when I would hold a grandson that looked like this same bundle of life. I felt that I would have another chance, through the grandchild that he would one day give me, to continue caring for my children as I'd wished I could have when I was younger.

That day never came, and it never will.

Journal

Journal

Chapter ② 2

May 8, 2009

On December 3, 1980, Vincent Joshua Weber entered my life. On May 8, 2009, he was gone.

To me, he was perfect, but I know Vincent struggled. He had a hard life. He had been born legally blind. His condition was neurological, and he shook all the time. He attended a special school for children who are disabled, where teachers and specialists who were trained in this field were able to work with him on his fine motor skills. With prayer and attention, he was able to do well, though life was still not easy for him. I eventually transferred him out of the school and put him into a Christian School. I also took Vincent to a specialist who designed exercises and special glasses that gave him the ability to see. In fact, with years of training and special eye exercises, he was able to function quite normally.

Nonetheless, as Vincent grew older, his symptoms returned and were stronger and quicker than we had anticipated. The shaking returned, and he often had difficulty walking without pain. This brought him a great deal of stress, which seemed to exacerbate his symptoms. The doctors suspected multiple sclerosis. I, too, had my fears and suspicions, but I never spoke of them—as if my silence would keep them away. Obviously, they did not.

Two weeks prior to Vincent's death, I felt the Lord speaking to me. I remember one conversation in particular, when God spoke to my heart while I was in the car, and I realized He was going to take Vincent home.

I remember thinking; *This has to be okay with me.*

I remember thinking, *God is asking me to release Vincent so His will can be done.*

I wept bitterly as I answered Him: "I understand, Father, and it is okay."

I understood that for Vincent, this would be glory; he would no longer suffer as he silently had for so long. He would be with the King, and his pain would be over. I also remember thinking this would be the hardest thing I had ever had to do. Though I was at peace, letting go was still so very difficult.

I realized that we are very fragile, weak vessels. Through difficult circumstances, we are given a deeper understanding—a fresh revelation—of what humility truly is.

I recognized the voice of the Lord when He spoke to me about Vincent, because I'd heard His voice before. For example, I had never really wanted to become a nurse, but I felt God spoke to my heart to suggest that I attend nursing school. I did so out of obedience to the Lord, though what I had always wanted to do was preach. In retrospect, I realize this was by His design, as I have had chances to do missionary work. These opportunities have opened doors for me to speak about Him that would have been closed otherwise. It's funny to me now as I look back. I visited places all over the Middle East and never once needed my nursing skills; however, my status as a nurse served as a cover for the real reason I traveled—to share the gospel.

I love the Lord with every fiber of my being. Pastoring the church in Danbury, Connecticut is very rewarding for me, and is an opportunity I would not have received if I hadn't attended nursing school and Bible College Though these venues I was able to travel to other countries and do missionary work. I have been blessed throughout my life to have many godly men and women speak into my life. They are the men and women who taught me what it meant to have godly character and not rush the process of growth that God himself teaches us each in a personal way when we follow hard after him. Such men and women as Fuschia Pickett and Irene Welch who was way beyond her years in the matters of worship and intimacy with God. These women saw the good in me, they were able to see God's plan for my life and helped to give me the tools I would need to pastor successfully. Others also have been wonderful mentors and teachers. I met many of them as I attended Bible College in Rochester, New York, an education I received that was funded by my career as a nurse. These were men and women who were sold out to the Holy Spirit and taught with such conviction the word of God. As a pastor Nick Welch taught the church in the things of God such as how to run after him and run relentlessly until as it were we caught him our beloved just as the shulamite girl ran after her beloved in the Song of Solomon. Another great mentor and teacher and father as it were to the church was Judson Cornwall .He was a gentle giant in the faith. A father and a teacher. Many books and teachings have come forth through these individual lives and I gleaned from them all. I am to say the least, a very blessed woman to have known and fellowshipped with them all.

Even in acknowledging this, I can truly say the real training I needed was in listening to the Holy Spirit; in hearing the voice of God. Our God is a God of providence, and nothing happens by mistake.

On the night of May 8, 2009, I was at my church getting ready for a service. My spiritual covering was visiting the church at that time. It is a very wise thing to have a covering to have someone that you are actually answerable to so that we don't veer off the straight path and cause others to fall that lean on and trust them. There are to many freewheeling men and women out there who woke up one morning and decided I think today I will pastor, it's a good career and there is a lot of money to be made. Well I guess that's true if that's what you want but I fear the Lord and would not take on such an awesome responsibility as to lead a people in the name of God had it not been for my calling and my convictions that I am truly exactly where I need to be in this day and hour. Any other man or woman who stands in the pulpit as a shepherd is a hireling, and when things get tough they leave the sheep and run. This causes the sheep to scatter and become prey to any lone wolf out there. From such a person run and don't look back. And as for me I certainly do not make a lot of money and I only have one true agenda that is to know him and to make him known.

Vincent was late in arriving that night. I had just seen him before I left for the church. We were together earlier, and we had stopped for gas. He would always pump my gas for me.

I remember thinking, "Of all days to be late, this is not the day!"

My mentor was visiting, and we needed to open the building to the congregation. I had given the church keys to my son, and his tardiness left us all outside until the assistant pastor arrived and was able to let us in.

Once inside, I rushed around, preparing for service. After several minutes, I approached my office and noticed a police officer by my door. I remember thinking "Wow, this is going to be a good meeting! Even the police are coming! And why not? I have a good, working relationship with them."

As I headed toward my office to greet them, I was met by the officer, who told me that I could not enter my office.

I remember telling the officer, "Oh it's okay; I'll only be a minute or two," but he was insistent that I not go in.

Puzzled, I introduced myself. "I'm Pastor Evelyn Weber, and this is my office ... "

I hadn't even finished the sentence when the officer's manner changed, and he quickly ushered me into my office.

As I entered the room, I took one look at my husband's face, at my pastor's face, and the faces of others in the office., We were packed out that night and we had many visiting ministry who had already arrived and were sitting in my office till things began and service actually started. As I approached the office and I saw the look on the faces of everyone there, and right then and there I knew. The worst thing that I could imagine had happened. What was just a fear in my heart had now become a reality to my eyes.

I turned immediately to my husband, William, and said "Don't make it easy. Just tell me which one it is." Remembering my conversation with the Lord, and I already knew which child it was, but I needed to hear it myself.

With the most incredible look of pain, my husband spoke the words.

"Vincent. It's Vincent."

Journal

Chapter ③

Happenstance and Providence

VOLUMES UPON VOLUMES ARE WRITTEN about grief recovery. Some explain how to overcome the void that remains after the death of a loved one; others, how to go on living as if nothing happened. Still more address how to deal with society when people are less than understanding of everyone's varying healing processes and the time frame for doing so. This book is about none of those things. I am not writing to talk about the death of my son. Since the beginning of time, millions upon millions have died, and millions more survivors have endured the anguish and feeling of utter helplessness as I just did at that very moment and yet they moved on in spite of that moment of complete despair and sorrow. Another self-help book on this topic is not needed, and this will not be the focus of the book you are now reading.

This book is a about a journey. I share with you the details of my son's death only to explain the journey to my suffering place, and the understanding I have gained after walking through it. My journey has been a ritualistic, repetitive process of dying to myself, of walking through a stinging fire that forged a new revelation in me so that Christ could emerge, through my life, as the hope of all glory.

One of many truths I have gained in this process is a new, profound understanding of humility.

I have seen people who, believing that God walks stooped over in a posture of earthly humility, have walked around imitating that position in a misconception of what humility truly is. They believe that walking stooped over somehow makes them holy or reverent or something. I have come to know that is not the case at all. That is a false humility.

After Vincent's death, in my own suffering place, weakness overtook me, causing me to lie prostrate in His presence. I would literally lie upon my son's grave and cry until I convulsed. In my grief, I was so weak I was often unable to stand. Still, I refused to allow myself to stand stooped over in my grief. Such a posture is one of defeat, and one I would never and could never assume.

Religious people might have a problem with that statement they may feel that I am being irreverent however it is the opposite. I have come to know that I am nothing without God and by this I mean to say that in my weakness, His strength was made perfect. In those moments, my strength was all but gone. Therefore, I placed no confidence in my own strength or my flesh. I found that I could be confident in His power, and that is what makes me strong. The apostle Paul explained that we are the circumcision, and that we worship God in the spirit, and that we are not to put any confidence in the flesh, but rather in the Lord Jesus Christ. I had sung about that Scripture as a child, but now my experience has given me a personal understanding. I have learned to live out this principle of living in His strength, not on my feet or even on my knees, but prostrate, on my face before Him.

How can I stand in this awesome place? In my grief, I have found Him to be as gentle as a dove, speaking words of comfort so powerful that my tears have immediately stopped. I have been left speechless, startled by the quiet of His awesome grace and love.

I mentioned previously that I know God spoke to me concerning the imminent death of my son. He was preparing me. I simply did not understand I had such little time left. It was not enough time to explain everything I wanted Vincent to know; how he was the reason I didn't give up when his biological father left, how I knew he called me his best friend, how I wanted him to know he was also mine.

Moments after I was told that Vincent had died, a woman from my congregation brought me a bouquet of hand-picked flowers from her garden. They were bleeding hearts—the flower of mourning. Ironically, she did not know in that moment that my son had died, nor could she have known earlier in the day, when she says the Lord spoke to her and told her that she should pick them for me.

As I received them, I thought to myself "Could God truly be so tender and attentive in my grief? Isn't there some diplomat, some king, someone more important who is to lose a child who deserves His attention?"

In that moment, I recognized firsthand that my God does not care about position. There is only one position He acknowledges, and that is the position of Christ Jesus nailed to the cross, His arms spread out wide to embrace the entire universe with the gift of grace; grace that covers our sins; grace that washed away all of Vincent's mistakes and failures. God receives His only Son with open arms, just as He carries us—as He carried my Vincent—to Him.

In those moments, I also began to understand the language of love God used as He had spoken to me over the previous two weeks. First, He told me what He was going to do. Second, He asked me to release my child to Him. Third, He sent my pastor—my mentor and my spiritual covering—halfway across the country to be with me at the moment I would learn the news. And finally, He had sent the flowers, the bleeding hearts—the mourning blooms.

How gentle and loving He was as He spoke to me. He was a gentleman. He was kind. He supernaturally provided for all the needs of the funeral, and He sent flowers. Those bleeding hearts; they were a poetic expression of His love.

Suddenly, in my sorrow, I realized: "This is the language of love—the overture of a bridegroom unto His bride."

This was the first lesson I learned on my journey to a place whose name I didn't know; a place called 'there.'

Journal

Journal

Chapter 4

The Train Ticket

THAT SAME EVENING, BEFORE I learned of Vincent's death, I had been on my way to a hotel to pick up my pastors, who were visiting at the time, for dinner. As I was driving, my sister called me. We had begun to talk, as sisters will, about all sorts of things, when for some reason we found ourselves upon the topic of losing a child.

I remember she had said, "I wonder, how do people live through this?"

I thought for a moment and recalled a story I had read about Corrie Ten Boom from her book *The Hiding Place*. *Corrie was a Jewish girl who lived in Poland during the time of the Holocaust.* She had been at a train stop with her father during World War II. She was frightened and shared her fears about going to the concentration camps with her father. She had this fear because her family helped the Jewish people hide in their home and the risk of being found out and sent to the concentration camps was a very real threat. One day while waiting for a train at the train station she asked her father what will happen to us if we are found out? "If we have to go, how will we be able to live through such a horrible trial?"

Her father thought for a moment, then held up the train ticket he had just purchased.

"Do you see this ticket?" he asked. "A little while ago, I did not have it because I did not need it. But just as I needed it, I was able to have it. That is what it is like to suffer. One thinks to themselves, 'How will I be able to endure this horrific tragedy?' but when they need it, God gives them the ticket."

Little did I know, as I shared this story with my sister, that in an hour and a half I would experience this phenomenon myself, receiving a ticket to endure the fiery trial that awaited me. Thinking back, I believe that God was speaking to me through my remembrance of that story. I was about to experience a most grave form of suffering, but He had the ticket I needed to pass through it. The memory of Corrie Ten Boom's story was reassurance that I would have what I needed to endure the trial ahead.

Several days prior to receiving the news of Vincent's death, I had been shopping for a member of our congregation who was to be ordained as a care pastor. I made the decision to buy him a prayer shawl as a token of the event, because I frequently use a prayer shawl in my 'soaking times'—sessions of prayer when I simply 'soak' in His presence. As I browsed the selection of prayer shawls in our local shop, I noticed a beautifully unique shawl emblazoned with flames all over it. The design struck me, because in my personal prayer time I had been asking for the fire of God, so I decided to purchase the shawl for myself.

The next day, as I put on my new prayer shawl, the Lord spoke to me very clearly.

"My daughter, I am going to bring you through a fiery trial, but it is for glory. Do not be afraid, for I am going to be with you."

I did not know what my trial would be, but I knew that journeys to our suffering places take us through fire, and that God would provide the ticket for the inevitable difficulty.

There is a tangible glory in the garment of praise God gives us in the midst of our fiery trial. It lifts the spirit of heaviness; it quenches the spirit of mourning. The Word tells us that weeping endures through the night, but that joy comes in the morning (Psalms 30:5). God will not leave us comfortless, and He will wipe away every tear.

I realize that the prayer shawl I purchased represented the covering I received from God in the secret, intimate place where God and I commune alone. In that place, there is resurrection power, power that has defeated death, the last enemy. With that victory, I know that my son will rise again, and I will forever be with him.

The flames encountered in my journey have been hot, but they have served as a purifying process. They were a way to bring my old nature to its knees for the purpose of God. We cannot serve such a mighty, powerful, awesome God and hope to do great exploits in His name before we fully understand who He is. Those people who truly know their God know first and foremost that He *is* God.

The Bible tells of a woman with an issue of blood who pressed through the crowd so that she could touch the hem of Jesus' garment. She had faith that if she could touch even His clothing, she would be healed. By her faith and persistence, she was instantly healed, and that absolute faith was credited to her as righteousness. Many pressed in on Him that day, but she touched Him with faith and with purpose.

I know myself, and I know that in my life I have run hard after God; I have pressed to know Him, and I know I am never satisfied with only the hem of His robes. On the day that I put on that prayer shawl, that fiery

Tallit, my God, who also knows me, covered me and held court with me as in the tabernacle. In His love and mercy, He met with me. To this day, when I pull on that shawl, I shake; not because I am afraid of God, but because He met me there. He warned me of the fire, because He did not intend to hurt me. He made His presence known because I listened.

In all of our trials, when hurt comes, He is there. While we are in the flesh, there will be hurt. Pain will come into everyone's lives, but He has said in His Word that He will never leave nor forsake us. We can hear His voice even now, saying, "Come to me and I will give you rest; rest from the fear of an unloving, unkind, or unmerciful God. I am meek in spirit. I love you with an everlasting love."

God loves us. He loves me, and He loves you. He will meet you in your trial—on the journey to your suffering place—with what you need to make it through. A royal exchange occurs when we realize that no matter the trial we face, we are not being punished. Christ was punished in our place. We must realize that if we desire to ride to the high places with God, we must often go to the lower places first.

In this truth, we can see that even death is an act of kindness and love on God's part. The Word says "Precious in the sight of the Lord is the death of his saints" (Psalm 116:15).

Death is precious, because once we have walked through the trial of life with Him at our side, we return to Him, to His presence, where we first began.

In my journey, I lost my Vincent, but I found this truth as I approached a place called 'there.'

Journal

Journal

Chapter 5

Restaurant Conversation

AFTER ENDING THE PHONE CALL with my sister, I continued to the hotel, where the pastors were waiting in the lobby. I was quite tired because I had been sick with pneumonia for a couple of months and had only recently begun to recover. I'd had very little rest because our church was in the midst of hosting a spring conference that many pastors, including my own, were attending at the time.

My pastors joined me in the car, and we drove to the restaurant. While at dinner, Gabriel who was my pastor and covering at that time said that he was excited for our church because it had grown so much that we were looking for a bigger building. While discussing this with the other pastors, I shared with Gabriel a vision that God had given me.

I was blessed to have a vision from God when I was in my early twenties—almost forty years prior to that night's conversation—that would set the course for the destiny that God had planned for me. I know now that it involved the entire Northeast, though at the time I did not realize the magnitude of it, nor that it would require much more of me than I had ever expected in order to fulfill it. It had taken nearly forty years to 'walk it out' and realize the full scope of what God had shown me.

Young men and women often think that when God gives a vision, it is immediate, for the present, for the 'here and now.' This is the case for some visions, but more often, if God gives a vision of any great magnitude, it will require years of preparation, and involve a long period of breaking and dying to the self, of extensive time on the proverbial 'potters wheel.' Many people enter into ministry unprepared, not yet having experienced (sometimes not even willing to experience), the learning and dying process, seeking only God's glory. These people often fall and fail early in their ministries. They have not yet experienced the growth that comes from taking a journey through their suffering place. They have yet to learn that the glory they seek is never their own. It is God's glory. They have yet to understand that the awesome privilege of serving the most high God in ministry will require that they die to themselves, exchanging their own identity for an identity in Him. It is indeed a painful process, an unpopular process, but one that is necessary to serve Him and to see the vision fulfilled.

As my pastor Gabriel began to talk to me about the ministry taking place in my church, I was reminded of the vision given to me in my youth, only now, I was able to speak to him from a new perspective, as if I was viewing a film in a theater and explaining the scenes to a blind man. I remember telling him that only one thing was lacking for the vision to be totally realized. He asked what it was, and so I shared.

There was a place in the vision where I approached an altar. Running across the altar was a rushing river, deep, rapid, and flowing swiftly. I remember the Lord asking me if I knew what that river was. I thought for a moment as I watched the river rush across the altar, then reached a conclusion. Confident in my summation, I answered the Lord.

"This must be the river of God."

In the years since giving God this answer, I have come to realize that God is never moved by our answers, especially when they are given as if we have discovered something that He never knew. He was not asking me the question for His benefit; He asked so that His revelatory wisdom would have the opportunity to penetrate my flesh, and understanding might come to my human brain.

God replied to my answer with these words: "No, it is not the river of God. It is your tears; you will cry rivers of tears for my people."

I confessed to my pastor that I was not yet at the point where I had cried rivers of tears for God's people. At times I had wept, but not in the way I had seen in the vision. I told my pastor that I had never been so broken as to weep like that, and I knew at some point I would have to be crushed. Little did I know that within the hour, I would be.

As I look back, I can see the providence of God in the timing of the pastors' visits. At the time, I did not know that my pastor had been weeping and interceding for someone for two weeks, not knowing for whom, but knowing only that a death was imminent. He later told me that he had feared for his own child at the time.

He had told his wife, "I do not know who it is, but there is going to be a tragic death; however, it will be for glory. We just have to walk through the pain process first.

Psalm 23:4 says, "Ye, though I walk through the valley of the shadow of death, I will fear no evil, for Thou art with me. Thy rod and Thy staff, they comfort me." My pastors unknowingly cried out for two weeks on my behalf, not knowing exactly who they were crying for. God, however, knew the inevitable. He knew what was coming, and prepared a garrison of mighty men and women of God to be with me, to stand completely encircled around me during this time.

I once read a book entitled *Don't Waste Your Sorrows* by Paul E. Billheimer. When you are brought to a place of sorrow, where you are crushed and then healed again, you are still weakened—forever broken. Anyone who has broken a bone knows that even long after it heals, it can easily be broken again. God wanted to bring me to such a place, not to hurt me, but to make me vulnerable and dependent upon Him. I have been made more pliable, and can quickly be taken to a place of vulnerability again by something as simple as a thought or a brief word from God. The difference now is that He can do so not just for my benefit, but for the sake of His people. Now the rivers can flow any and every time God sees fit to use me. I have vowed not to waste this painful process, and to allow God to use it for His glory.

God crushes only that which is fully matured; developed to the point that transformation is necessary for it to be of further use. Grapes, when they have matured, are crushed to make fine wine. Only the mature roses are crushed to make the sweet-smelling fragrances of perfume. Olives must be ground, crushed, and pressed so that their oil comes forth to be strained and sifted to remove its impurities. Mature seeds and flowers are crushed and blended with crushed, mature olives to make anointing oil. As with all of these natural things, the by-product of our personal, spiritual, and emotional crushing is to transform us, to bring out the qualities necessary to function as a vessel for God's anointing. Crushing will forever cure us from moving in our own strength, because our form is changed by the power of God. It inserts us into a process of being changed by the Master's hand. We must be purified so that we do not taint His glory.

In 2 Samuel, Chapter 6, we read that Uzzah died when he touched the cart that carried the Ark Of The Covenant, even though he did so to prevent it from falling. I used to think God's apparent outburst was unfair until I did a study and found that 'Uzzah' means 'man's own strength.' We are crushed and changed so that we can move in God's strength rather than our own.

Qoheleth (the son of David and writer of Ecclesiastes), who refers to himself as 'The Preacher' throughout his book, muses in Chapter 1, verse 2, "'Vapor of vapors, and futility!' says the Preacher. 'Vapor of vapors and futility of futilities! All is vanity!'" Vanity, in this context, translates to 'emptiness, falsity, or vainglory.' In our own strength, we are apart from

God, and without Him we are nothing more than a vapor in the wind. We can do nothing without the touch of the Master's hand.

Romans 8:20 says it like this: "For the creation (nature) was subject to futility (condemned to frustration), not because of some intentional fault on its part, but by the will of him who is subject to it. Yet with hope."

In response to all of this, Romans 8:28 reads, "All things work together for good for those who love Him and are called according to His purposes." God is a restoring God. He allows things that are dear to us to be taken away; not to destroy us, but to perfect us. God also gives back, and in greater measure than He allows us to experience loss. Vincent was taken from me. Through that loss, God has fashioned me for the purpose of bettering my ministry to His people.

I will embrace Vincent again someday, and that will last for all eternity. I envision him at times; sometimes as a young boy at the gates of heaven, waiting for his dearly missed and beloved mother, other times as a soldier coming home from a long war. I often envision the reunion as train doors opening and my son frantically running toward me, unable to bear another second apart. This will be my heaven—the exchange of all the love in him for all the love in me. I know that in eternity, all that has been taken will be restored, perfectly and forever.

I have come to know God as my loving Father, my daddy. When I was a little girl, I was so taken with my earthly daddy. He was tall and handsome, and he made me feel safe. I would stand on the top of his feet and we would dance, or rather, he would dance and swirl around as I was taken wherever he stepped. I thought I wanted to marry my daddy. I'm sure most little girls have felt this way about their earthly daddy. When I see my heavenly Daddy, I would like to think I will feel the same way. I would like to think I could get on top of his feet and swirl around all of heaven with Him. My heavenly Daddy—the Daddy of the entire universe—will make all things right. The rivers of tears will be washed away, and I will forever be in complete joy and at peace; but for now, what a privilege to be considered for the fire. What a privilege to be noticed by the King. How special to know that He trusted me with a vision.

God is my Father. He takes notice of me. He provides for me, even when I do not see my own need. He crushes that He may purify, and He restores that He may be glorified. This is the nature of the great and majestic God I serve, and I would not have known these things had I not yielded in this journey through my suffering place on the road to a place called 'there.'

Journal

Chapter 6

Melted Identity

Ephesians 4:11 says "He himself appointed and gave men to us, some to be apostles, prophets, pastors, evangelists and teachers."

I believe there is no greater work than that of the ministry; however, this is a job for which one cannot apply. When God needs ministers, nowhere is there an ad posted that says "Apostles, prophets, pastors, evangelists, and teachers wanted!" God does not solicit for these positions. He appoints them. But for what are they appointed, and why is this His way of filling the need for them?

Each office serves a function. Apostles are special messengers. Prophets are inspired preachers who expound upon the word of God. Evangelists are spreaders of the gospel, often as traveling missionaries. Pastors are like shepherds, tending and caring for the needs of their 'flock' or congregation. Teachers study and share what they learn to help make the Word of God clear and plain to us. God's intention in appointing people to these offices is to equip the saints, His consecrated people, to build up Christ's body, the church. His desire is that His people develop until everyone attains unity in the faith. He longs for His children to have a full and accurate knowledge of the Son of God. Our Father wants us to grow in maturity, to develop a complete personality that mirrors the standard of Christ's own perfection. He wants us to find our completion in Him. When these things are in place, we are no longer children tossed about like ships, listing to and fro with each chance gust of teaching, wavering with every changing wind of doctrine. Without stability and direction, we fall prey to the cunning and cleverness of unscrupulous men; gamblers engaged in every form of trickery. God has appointed His leaders so that His children may learn more of Him, and not be led astray.

In this way, I did not choose God. He chose me. Therefore, I do not get to do things my own way. I have had to yield to His authoritative structure of leaders who have taught and trained me in the ways of God. God Himself designed and prepared a course of teaching for me. God Himself has decided the path that I will take. God alone works on my character. God alone shows Himself to me in all things. God alone teaches me how to go to war. God alone causes me to leap over a wall and defeat my enemies.

When I have been sick, God has shown me that He is my healer. When I have been hungry, God has shown me that He is my provider. It is God alone who sticks closer to me than a brother. God is my comforter, my friend, and my deliverer. He is a providential God who provides for my needs long before they become a prayer of petition in my mouth. When I have been forsaken by many I have known, God alone gave me faith to believe; to trust in His Word rather than the voices of those around me.

Before ever saying 'yes' to the invitation to serve God as a minister of the gospel, we first must realize that it is God alone who calls. Then, we need to understand that God's way up is down. A limp most assuredly comes with the call. Brokenness, persecution, and rejection are all part of preparation to serve as a minister. We must know God if we are to serve Him, and to know Him, we must also partake in His suffering. If we are to reign with Him, then we must suffer with Him. He was wounded for our transgressions, and was bruised for our iniquities. He was the chastisement of peace. He was despised and rejected by men all for our sakes, and we must have our part in this if we expect to move in the miraculous ways He did.

All of this will cause our self-centeredness to fade. Our identity must go in order for us to be identified with Christ. This is a necessary work wrought by the Master Himself.

I remember when I said yes to the Lord and His call. I was immediately moved to a new location—taken away in the providence of God. The very first night in my new locale, I had a prophetic dream. In my dream, the Lord woke me by calling my name. I rose from my bed and ran to the voice, and found Him standing before me. I drew closer to Him, and He began to speak to me. He told me He was pleased that I had left all I that I had to follow Him so that He could fulfill His plan for my life.

He said, "I am so very pleased with you and the decision that you made, and I have a gift for you." He continued, saying, "I have the gift of a contrite heart for you."

I was excited to receive a gift from the Lord, yet I did not know what a contrite heart was.

The next morning, I ran to my pastor to tell him what had happened. When I boasted that I had been given the gift of contriteness, I was surprised when he groaned as if having just received bad news. He explained to me that a contrite heart is a remorseful, penitent, and repentant heart; a crushed heart, like a fine powder.

I thought for a moment and decided that if a contrite heart comes from God, then it will be good for me.

I said to myself, "This is a good thing! This will qualify me to minister!"

If God calls you, then God trains and qualifies you. Part of that training is education. (2Tim.2:15), "Study to show thyself approved of God; a workman not needing to be ashamed, being able to rightly divide the word of truth."

Heresy, ignorance, arrogance, and pride are byproducts of disallowing God to have His way in our lives. He must be allowed to season us. Then and only then can we lose our identity in Him. Do not shortchange yourself from being blessed by the Father. No one else can bless you.

Years later, the Lord spoke to me again.

"Evelyn, do you ever wonder why it was I gave you a contrite heart?"

I replied, "Yes Lord, I do. I do often."

He said "Then let me tell you. A broken vessel can be put back together again. They can become as good as new, and you can hardly tell that there was ever a break there. They resemble exactly what they were, but when a man or a woman allows me to give them a contrite heart, those are the precious vessels that I crush. Once I crush them, they become like powder; like a powder you would put on your face. That powder cannot become what it once was, because it has lost all identity. I can then take that person and apply them to myself so that when they minister, men do not see them, but rather they see me. They see Jesus in them, and only Jesus."

All identity; all that represented who I was before is no longer who I am. I am a new creation in Christ. If Christ calls us, He causes us to lose our identity and take on the character of Christ. This changes our character, but we do not become robots. When we are changed, we are enhanced in our own God-given personalities, which were given to us by God at birth. When we release our identity, we are sanctified and become the workmanship of His hands.

Many people who are not yet prepared have come to me, wanting my ministry to use them in some way. Often they say, "You need me, pastor! I have an anointing that can bless you and grow your ministry!" This saddens me so very much. Taking such an approach is like prostituting their gifts.

To such people I say, "Your anointing and gifts were given to you at your salvation, but in order for your gifts to be used here, what I need to see is your character develop into the fullness of the character of Christ. Otherwise, your character will cause you to forfeit the gifts, and you will fall, and cause others to fall."

Paul wrote in Galatians 2:20, "For I live, never the less not I but Christ lives in me."

Paul lost his identity. And we who are ministers or who desire to become ministers need to realize that we must also do the same. We must lose who we are in order to reflect who he is.

In my journey, I have learned that my identity must fade. It must melt away so that I can better serve Him when I emerge from my suffering place into a place called 'there.'

Journal

Chapter 7

Developing the Character of David

THE BOOK OF I CHRONICLES details a process by which King David becomes a new man. David decided to bring the Ark of the Covenant back to Israel that it might be seen by the eyes of the people. Beginning in Chapter 13, verses 5 through 11, we read of a celebration that accompanied the moving of the ark, but the celebration ended badly. It is evident in David's reaction that while his heart was certainly in the right place, his character was in need of more development.

In the process of moving the ark, Uzzah, one of David's men, put his hand out to protect the ark from falling as it was pulled across the difficult terrain. At the very moment Uzzah touched the ark, he was struck dead. Verse 11 is a telling moment. It reveals that David was offended when the Lord struck down Uzzah. He was so offended that he named the place 'Perez-Uzzah,' which means 'The Outburst Against Uzzah.' David was so distraught that he abandoned his plans to move the ark and left it in the house of Obed-Edom. Until Uzzah was struck dead, King David's identity was in himself. His trust at that time was still in his own efforts. This is evident in his decision to delay the return of the ark to Jerusalem for three months.

The word *uzzah* means 'man's own effort.' As ministers and as Christians, we must learn it is most important that we not take our positions for granted and move into the realm of our own efforts. Many men and women of God are delayed in fulfilling their calling because they try, through their own efforts, to carry out their godly instructions. This process almost always ends with the death of their visions.

At the point when Uzzah was stricken, David's identity was misplaced. Dr. Ron Cottle explores this in his book *Anointed To Reign.* He was known as David the Great; a mighty man who had defeated giants. He was David the Warrior. He was David the Shepherd Boy who cared for his sheep. His identity was still in his earthly accomplishments. A shepherd was a good thing to be; so was a warrior, but 'king' was God's ultimate title for David. David was sure to become king, but only if he listened to the Lord.

There are men and women who have gone to their graves without attaining God's ultimate goal for their lives, because they did not learn through their processes what humility truly was. They did not learn that the only true confidence they should have had was in God.

David's change began when he learned to fear God. Over the course of three months, David realized God's power and sovereign authority over him, and finally asked God how he could safely bring the ark of God home to Jerusalem. God had a perfect plan for this task. The return of the ark was not accomplished by David's plans, but rather by God's when David humbled himself and asked.

How often we could avoid pain if only we would ask the Lord for His plans rather than making our own. I have learned that I should never try, in my own strength, to fulfill God's call. He will fulfill His call in my life. I must submit and do it His way, not mine. My own efforts are flawed. The place called 'there' is where He rests, just as His presence rested in the Ark of the Covenant. I want to be able to worship there, in that intimate place. I do not want to lose my place in His presence, and so I willingly have exchanged my own identity for His identity.

Isaiah 33:13 reads, " 'Hear ye, who are far off,' says the Lord, 'what I have done; and you who are near, acknowledge my might.'"

I can acknowledge His might only when I am enmeshed with Him; when I melt into who He is. Mountains can only be moved when God is our shelter and our resting place.

Strength comes from humility and intimacy in a place called 'there.'

Journal

Chapter 8

Jehova Rophica; My Healer

When a person experiences tragedy, they often go into shock. When this happens, they are prone to behave strangely. Kingdom living is different. When Vincent passed away, the Spirit of God rose up within me, causing me to behave in a way that was indeed out of the ordinary, yet which was completely godly and not a 'shock' response. If anything, I was 'shocked' into the presence and the ways of God.

It is amazing what we will endure when we say 'yes' to God, and accept the deep training He will require of us to find Him. For years prior to Vincent's death, I had experienced a period of sanctification. For twenty years, I was intensely trained and sanctified by God. During this time, God took me through a process of diminishing myself to such a degree that the only things I owned as a tangible testament to my existence on Earth was a coat rack containing a few articles of clothing.

At the time this portion of my process began, I was a telephone counselor for *The 700 Club*. I was a woman in a new city. My husband had recently left me as a single mother to my four children, and we were living in a single-wide trailer. Life, it seemed at the time, could not have been any more difficult. I was also a nursing student, going to school during the day and spending the rest of the time with my children. In the midst of all this, I said 'yes' to God and His call, and He took me up on it. It was in this hectic season that I learned God was *Jehovah Rophica,* my Healer.

My son Nicholas was a strong, tough young man; the kind who seemed determined to try everything possible to turn my hair gray long before I'd earned a silver crown. Nicholas had joined the football team as an outlet for his various energies, and arrived home one evening complaining of pain in his finger. Initially, we shrugged it off as a simple injury from playing a rough sport. I told him to stop playing so rough and give it a rest, yet he still complained for several days of pain in his finger, so on that Friday afternoon, we visited a doctor. Routine x-rays revealed that Nicholas' finger was broken. The doctor wrapped his finger and told us it would heal on its own. On Monday I received an unexpected call from the doctor, requesting that I come back in with Nicholas. Concerned, I left school early, picked Nicholas up, and we returned to the doctor's office. As we sat and waited to see the physician, I knew the news could not be good, but I was grievously unprepared for what the doctor would say.

The doctor entered the room and began straight away.

"I have shown Nicholas' x-rays to my colleagues, and we agree that Nicholas has cancer, a variety called squamus cell cancer."

He went on to explain that it was an aggressive cancer. Based on the x-ray, Nicholas was already missing a knuckle that the doctor presumed had been eaten away by the disease.

I was completely numb. As I recovered, I asked what we needed to do. My doctor replied that his colleagues would help him decide upon a course of treatment.

I went home with my son that night and tried to behave as if it was nothing too serious, but I was sick. I did not know what to do, so I did the only thing I could. I fell on my face and wept before God.

"Father, please don't let Nicky die!" I cried. "I can't take anymore loss! I can't see him suffer! Please, God; heal him. Please! You can do anything. I know you are Jehovah Rophica. Please, God, heal my son!"

Once all the kids went to bed, I continued to weep until I fell asleep. The next morning, I got up for school and continued to pray all day long. I had no one else to turn to, as I was alone and in a new place. I had only God, my Father. I learned years later that as I was driving to work, praying and crying out to God, Nicholas too was on his knees asking God to spare him, and to do so for my sake, because he felt his mom could take no more heartache.

After work, I came home, spent a short time visiting with my children, finished cleaning the supper dishes, and then called my pastor's wife and told her the news.

"God is faithful," she said, "and He will do what only God can do. Trust in Him."

She always pointed to Jesus. She was a great help, teaching me to look to Jesus alone as my source of help. To this day, I am thankful that with the help of her example, I have learned to lean on the Rock of Ages. I know from experience that He is faithful in all things—in life and in death as well.

Even with her support, it was a difficult week, living in the unknown. Not until Nicky's next appointment would we know what needed to be done and how it would happen. Sunday came, and like every Sunday, we went to church. I remember the worship portion of the service being particularly good that day, but all the while I suffered alone with an ache in the pit of my stomach. I had told no one of Nicholas' condition because I did not know what to say, as we were still waiting for the next appointment.

Communion was a scheduled part of the service that Sunday, and as worship ended, before we sat down for the sermon, my pastor's wife stepped to the podium to pray over that portion of the service. I was completely taken by surprise when she began her prayer by calling out to God on behalf of my son.

"Father God," she began. "Even as we take the blood and body of Christ, we remember that He died that Nicky would be healed, and I ask you to heal him."

What happened next was so spontaneous and powerful I could hardly believe it. The dancers in the church began to dance around my son, as in a dance of warfare for his healing. The musicians then began to play music, as if it was a type of war march. I fell to my face, as I realized it was a move of the Holy Spirit. God was in the room. His presence was so heavy that I could not raise my head.

Afterward, Nicholas said he felt heat travel down his finger. He told me he felt all the pain leave, and he felt fine.

The next morning I called the doctor and asked if I could bring Nicholas for an appointment, and the next morning we arrived at the office. Once we were in the examination room, I asked the doctor if he would check Nicholas one more time. He agreed to perform another x-ray, which I am sure he did only to please me. With the process completed, the doctor examined the films and was amazed by the result. The picture clearly displayed an entirely new finger, knuckle and all. The God I serve had dramatically demonstrated His power as Jehovah Rophica—God, my Healer.

In this instance, my journey affected at least two others. The doctor, who witnessed Nicholas' instant recovery, gave his heart to the Lord. I had the privilege of worshiping with him in church for many years. Also, in addition to my son's healing, a foundation was laid in him, and he now pastors a church in Asheville, North Carolina. Others, many others, will be affected by our journey through our suffering place on the way to a place called 'there.'

Journal

Journal

Chapter 9

Jehova Jireh; My Provider

Raising a family as a single woman, without the covering of a husband, is a unique challenge. Raising a family alone brings about a different batch of needs and requires a different set of rules. There are many lessons I had to learn, and many things I had to learn to do in a different way. In this season of adjustment, I came to know God as *Jehovah Jireh;* God, my Provider.

Our life as a family had changed, and I quickly came to learn that God was already aware of our changing needs. He was already prepared to provide accordingly. It was sometimes easy to forget that He looks in advance and knows what we need long before we know we have a need.

God placed in my heart a strong desire to tithe faithfully. I wanted to please my heavenly Father in this way because I love him so. I wanted to walk in a manner that was upright and obedient. For this reason, tithing was never a question for me. Every week, the first thing I budgeted was our tithe. Financially, God came first and my needs were second. The bills were always paid, even if they were occasionally late. My children never starved. Our needs were always met, despite how hard it got at times.

One night, I remember speaking with my mother about our financial situation. She had called me and after speaking together for a while, I shared with her that I did not have any food and did not know what I was going to do. My mother immediately responded that she did not understand why I gave so much money to the church when my family was about to starve. I told her that we were not starving, and explained that I was not giving my money to the church, but to God. I was not asking the church to do what God had promised He would do. The call quickly ended, and I said goodnight and went to bed.

After the children and I moved from a singlewide trailer we lived in a two-bedroom apartment. At that time I did not have my own bedroom. And I slept on a cot in the living room, but it was very comfortable. That night, after the call with my mother, I said goodnight to the children, closed their doors, turned out the lights, and began to weep as I lay on my cot. Not knowing what else to do, I prayed.

"Father, you heard my conversation with my mom. I know I could ask the church for help, but I need to know that it is you who will take care of me. I am not going to ask anyone for help."

I then cried myself to sleep.

The next morning, I gave the children breakfast and asked them to pray with me before they left for their day, as we did every morning. I told them goodbye, and added that they should be excited for dinner, because we were going to have the best supper they had ever eaten. I knew there was no more food, but I knew God would not fail me. I then left for work, not knowing how God would provide for us, but had I given my concern to Him, and I knew He would be faithful.

My family and I lived on the second floor of our apartment building. I had a neighbor on the second floor, to which I had given a key to our apartment so she could let the kids inside when they arrived home from school. That day, however, the children were going to be home late, and I was excited that I would be home before them. I arrived home, quickly opened the door, and was amazed to see my living room piled with boxes upon boxes of food; hundreds of dollars worth of food, and a small note. The note read simply, "In the name of Jesus."

I screamed with joy. I wept and danced at the faithfulness of God.

I ran to my neighbor and asked her who had delivered all of the food. She told me that two old women had come and knocked at her door, asking if she knew the woman that lived in my apartment. She answered that she did, and when she heard what they were doing, she had used her key to let them in.

How did these women know of my need? The answer was simple. God is faithful. He heard my cry. God is faithful in all things, and He hears us when we cry.

Many times I have seen miracles like this. I have lived a life of faith, and could write volumes on how He has provided for my needs in this way.

At one point I was driving a car with balding tires, but I could not afford to replace them, so I asked my heavenly Father for help. A short time after my prayers, I was driving home and got a flat. In my frustration, I sat on the side of the road with my child and wept. A man from a house across the street came and asked if he could help me. I sobbed that I'd had a rough day and everything was going wrong, and while I appreciated his offer of help, I had no spare tire for him to change. He insisted he could help, and told me to pull into his driveway and sit with his wife for a while so he could try to fix my tire. I had no other options, so I agreed.

I sat and drank iced tea with his wife for nearly an hour before the man came in and told me he had fixed my flat. I said goodbye and thanked the couple, then walked to the driveway to find I had four brand new tires on my car. The man who had offered to help owned a tire store, and happened to have four tires of just the right size in his home garage. Again, God was faithful.

Another time, I was shopping in a town far from home when my four children and I were caught in a terrible storm. As we were driving, a very large limb fell right in front of our car, which I drove over and consequently punctured the oil tank. Again, I was stranded and wept on the side of the road. After several moments, I gathered my children and we knocked on someone's door to ask if we could use their telephone. At that point, we found that we were stranded for the evening due to the violent storm, and we became unintentional house guests. The next morning, the man of the house gave us a ride home, keeping the car and offering his help to have it repaired. Unbeknownst to me, he was a mechanic and owned a garage, where he repaired my car.

What a wonderful God I serve. He is Jehovah Jireh, the Great Provider, whom I've met on my journey to a place called 'there.'

Journal

Journal

Chapter 10

When You Don't Know What to Do, Sing

PEOPLE UNNECESSARILY SACRIFICE SO MUCH to gain the favor of God. In some countries, people practice rituals where they crawl on glass and beat themselves, doing great harm to their bodies as a sacrifice to God, when all God asks us to sacrifice is our praise. He asks that we sing praises to Him. He asks that we love Him.

I am amazed at how a sports stadium is full for every game of every football season. Fans pay large sums of money to attend the games and act absolutely crazy. They take off their shirts and paint themselves with their team colors. They scream and waive big foam hands, and make all sorts of noises just to be heard by their team. This is a picture of the sacrifice of praise for which He is asking! He is looking for a people that will pay whatever price to get closer to Him. Certainly, doing so will cost us something. It will cost our dignity. It will cost us our popularity if we are labeled a fanatic, but what we receive in exchange is well worth it.

I have been called a zealot. I personally consider that the greatest thing anyone has ever called me. I have been treated unkindly by my relatives. I have been beaten. I have been spit upon because of my love for the Lord Jesus Christ. The true reason for this mistreatment is the vision of Jesus people have seen in me. Sometimes the light of the Lord is so bright, the Enemy can stand it no more. No one in their right mind would enjoy this variety of suffering, even if it is done together with Christ. Neither do I. Even great men like the apostle Paul certainly did not enjoy being persecuted. I think of my suffering as a barometer to measure how I am doing with God. If people begin to like me too much, I begin to think that perhaps I am backsliding. I certainly do not seek to make enemies, nor do I make myself purposefully obnoxious. However, when I made a decision to become a savoring salt and a light on a hill, I expected such treatment to happen.

When I was in college, I learned a great lesson. Delayed gratification is more rewarding than instant gratification. How I learned this lesson is less important now than the truth of what I learned. Satan offers instant gratification. He offers the opportunity to experience now, without maturity and without responsibility, the things God would have us wait to experience until we are mature and crushed and sanctified unto Him. Satan gives instant power to his followers. This is why occult religions are growing at such a rapid rate. Immature and lawless members of the church have come to accept anything as being from God that gives them a spiritual high. So much has been sacrificed that God has been decreased and made such a small entity, all for our lack of patience.

I have learned to wait for God. He is faithful, and as in many things, it is much better to wait. The journey through our suffering place is one of waiting. He rewards those who wait; who persevere. He rewards the patient faithfulness of those who seek Him. I wait for God, and I am satisfied. In the end, I will embrace eternity with the assurance that I am a child of the most High God, The Great God Jehovah. He is my great reward.

I have found that when I am lost, and at a point where I feel anxious, or impatient, or do not know what to do, I can sing. I can sing His praises. I can sing, and I can wait on Him. Each time I sing, He meets with me. He touches my heart, and He gives me hope. On the night Vincent died, I could have left the church and gone home to be alone and mourn. I was so filled with pain and anguish that my son, my baby, was dead at only twenty-eight years old, but I had said 'yes' to God. For all of these years leading up to the loss of Vincent, I had been learning from the Master Himself who God my Father was. He is the God who takes so that he may give back in greater measure.

I stayed behind that night at the church .I stayed behind again as they rolled my sons lifeless body out of my home to place him into the hearse. Both times, I did the only thing I knew I could do. I sang. I sang for hours, and as I sang, the strength I needed was there. Each time I sang, I gained the strength to make the next step in my journey, and I moved. Every time I go to the cemetery to visit Vincent, I sing. I sing his favorite song—"Great is Thy Faithfulness," and every time, my Father comforts me.

I know that in eternity I will again have my son. He will no longer be sick, no longer be weak, and all that so easily beset him in life will be no longer. He will see with perfect eyes, and he will be filled with complete joy, peace and satisfaction.

I have shared this because for some, the journey is hard. For some, it seems unbearable. For some, it is so painful it seems impossible. I hope to make plain that for all who will say 'yes' to the call of God, we will share in some measure of His suffering. We will walk through a suffering place. Nonetheless, as we reach a place called 'there,' it will be worth every moment, even if the satisfaction is not immediate.

Journal

Chapter 11

Were You There?

IN THE FIRST FEW MONTHS after Vincent's death, I missed him so badly that it was painful for me. I cried for hours each day without stopping. I remember one particularly difficult morning. As I was pouring my coffee and praying, I began to weep bitterly.

I cried out "Holy Spirit, where were you? Why could you not prevent this awful tragedy? How could you allow this?"

In that moment, I could not imagine the Holy Spirit allowing someone, something, to crush my child and steal the life from my core.

"How could you? Where were you? Where were you when Vincent died? Why did he have to die alone? Why didn't you do anything to save him?" I cried.

I was desperate for an answer, for some understanding of where the Holy Spirit was at the moment when Vincent died. I was troubled at the thought that he had died alone, with seemingly no one to comfort him; no one to speak soft words of hope; no one to tell him of the pending ecstasy of heaven that awaited him.

The Spirit answered gently with words that will forever be a healing salve to me.

"I was there to catch him when he fell. I told you that I had to bring him home. I asked you to release him, and you did. When he was gone, I was there. I caught him as he fell into eternity. I took Vincent to the Father, where he is now free of pain, free of sickness, free of the fear of failure."

In the moment that I received this answer, all fear and anguish left me. I began to worship God again. Who was I to question? Why would I think for a moment that God would leave Vincent all alone? The Holy Spirit was there, waiting to catch him and carry him to the Father, into eternity. Even as the Spirit ushered Christ into the presence of His Father, even as He escorted Him into the presence of an applauding, angelic host, the same Spirit ushered my son into the Father's embracing arms. In revealing this to me, He also ushered the overwhelming sadness out of my heart.

Scripture speaks of God as an ever-present help in times of need. I have found this to be true. If we listen, we can hear him speaking to us. We can hear His words of comfort. I hold onto His words to get me through my day-to-day.

Crisis causes us to take notice of where we are. It makes us aware of every moment. It focuses us on enjoying those around us. Our perspectives change. I now view life with a fresh humility. I have always known my flesh was weak, but now I understand the passage that says, "Let the weak say I am strong" (1 Corinthians 4:10). My strength is not in me.

In our youth, we feel invulnerable. We rarely think of a time when we will grow old and need someone else's strength. Since Vincent's death, I have come to learn that my day-to-day strength is not my own. I draw from the well of life everyday. Jesus is that well, and by His strength, I can continue to live.

Jesus told Peter, "When you were young, you went your own way; but there will come a time when you grow old and others will lead you."

Jesus was referring to Peter's death on the cross. When my son died, a part of me died as well. I became a weak vessel needing to be led around. Through this process, I have become a person solely dependent upon God. When I am in His presence, I can feel His breath coming into me.

Our suffering and sorrow will feel like a fleeting moment in the light of eternity. Satan is a liar. He is a tormentor, and the closer we get to God, the more he will try to knock us down. He hates us because we now have the privilege that he forfeited long ago. We were created to praise, to worship, and to have intimacy with God. We are His ambassadors here on earth, and we will reign with Him forever. No wonder Satan hates us so much.

The Bible tells us that each and every one of us is fearfully and wonderfully made (Psalm 139:14). God does not make garbage. We are special to God, and He will not leave us. He will not forget us anymore than a mother can forget her nursing child. God is mindful of us every second, no, every nanosecond of every day. When we are born, He has already planned our lives, including the moment we will return to Him. Death has no sting when we know God. He keeps a heavenly account of all that concerns us.

Job 11:6 says, "You will surely forget your trouble, recalling it only as waters gone by."

How trivial life will seem in the realm of eternity, when we have walked our journey and arrived at a place called 'there.'

Journal

Chapter 12

The Dark Night of the Soul

THESE ARE TROUBLING TIMES IN which we live. Our country is troubled, and our economy is in turmoil. Millionaires literally lose their fortune overnight. The stock market has become unstable, as the number of people standing in welfare lines and unemployment lines have increased. Foreboding news is splashed all over the television. Earthquakes are occurring frequently all over the world. Health care reform is causing a panic in our country. The elderly are about to have Medicare taken from them. Children go to bed hungry every night. Sex trafficking has increased worldwide. Children are being exploited in ways that are unmentionable. Fear has increased in the hearts of all men, and hope has decreased. Little boys who are of elementary school age are being taught in school how to put on condoms. Righteousness is called evil while evil is confused with godliness.

The dark night of the soul is a refining process—a process of fire—through which one must go. All things will change in the fire. Many people speak of "waiting for the fire," but the fire is already here. When Jesus walked the earth, many did not realize that the Messiah was already among them. Likewise, in this time, the fire has already been here. The process has already begun. Only God can take us through the fire, and only God can bring us out.

The dark night of the soul prepares us for revival.

Scripture tells us that the whole earth moans and groans for the manifestation of the sons of God (Romans 8:22–23). If ever the earth was moaning, it is happening now.

In the fairy tale *Sleeping Beauty*, Princess Aurora fell asleep for one hundred years until the prince found her and kissed her on the lips. When she was awakened, the whole earth that had slept with her, sharing her death-like state, began to wake up. The trees sprouted green leaves, and flowers began to bloom. The birds appeared and sang a new song. The mountains lost their drab appearance, and the gray skies turned into rivers of aqua blue. White clouds appeared upon a sun-drenched canvas background. This is similar to God's description of how things will be in the last days. The sons and daughters of the Most High God will be made manifest. At that moment, the deliverance for which the earth awaits will appear as a sign of His returning with a sign of the bride beginning to reign with Him. The earth will shake off her slumber, and things will appear, as they should be. God has called us to be joint heirs with Him; to rule with Him on this reawakened earth. We will then have the fullness of understanding of the Scripture that reads, "Thy Kingdom come, Thy will be done, on earth as it is in Heaven" (Matthew 6:10).

In order to partake in such light and glory, we must surrender all control to the Master in the dark night of the soul. The dark night of the soul is a time of deeply painful experience. This place is like the womb. It is the place where we are fearfully and wonderfully formed into the image of Christ. As we walk through the dark night, we are taken deeper in our walk with God.

Many chase after gifts and outward manifestations of the Holy Spirit; few are willing to meet God in the dark night of the soul. They run like cowards at the thought of the fire purging their selfishness and self-seeking purposes from them. Many seek gifts, but it is the Gift Giver they should seek, because He is the Pearl of Great Price, and He is found only in the dark night of the soul.

When I walked through my dark night, I was irrational. Nothing appeared as it was. Nothing seemed to satisfy me. I was unable to explain to anyone the pain I was spiritually experiencing. They would not have understood. My pain was personal and internal. There was no way to articulate my suffering in mere words. My process was specific to me. As difficult as it was, I am grateful that God, in His sovereignty, brought me to my suffering place and through my dark night.

Unless a seed falls into the ground and dies, it cannot live. This death process, this dark night of the soul, takes away our ability to stand-alone. We become totally dependent on Him. To know and experience the joy of the morning, we must be willing to go through the night.

Jonah experienced his dark night of the soul while in the belly of a whale. Job experienced his dark night as he lost his family and fortune. Shadrach, Meshach, and Abednego experienced their dark night of the soul in the fiery furnace. In all of these situations, the Lord met them in their trial—in the desperation of their dark night.

It is the dark night of the soul that prepares us for revival.

A.W. Tozer spoke of the dark night of the soul in his book *The Spirit Filled Life*. "Remember how they nailed Jesus to the cross. Remember the darkness, the hiding of the father's face. This was the path that Jesus took to immortal triumph. As He is, so are we in this world."

The dark night of the soul is an inward process. It cannot be found outside of us. It happens deep within, in a place others cannot understand. It happens in a place where a love language passes between God and us. It happens in a place where the Holy Spirit waits to meet us. It is here, in our dark night, that we exchange our lives for His all; and it is here with us that He is the most comfortable.

You cannot kill what is already dead. Once we have walked through our dark night, we become fearless and terrible, a force with which to be reckoned. We are marked—initiated, if you will—into the terrible army of the Most High God, the Great Jehovah.

The apostle John said the dark night of the soul prepares us to live in the light.

Nothing lives until it dies. In order for us to have Christ in us, we must no longer exist. After my dark night, I am no longer who I was. He now lives in and through me. When one enters into the dark night of the soul, they die. The shell continues, but what lives inside is God Himself.

We live in difficult times; times we did not choose. Likewise, we cannot choose our dark night of the soul. God chooses for you. The dark night of the soul is the last place in our journey before we experience victory. It is here that the vision is realized. It is at this last, most difficult stage that we experience the resurrection power of Christ Jesus. When God sends us into our dark night, we have nearly reached a place called 'there.'

Journal

Journal

Chapter 13

Conclusion

THE WONDERFUL THING ABOUT A vehicle's navigation system is it consistently helps you to find your way back home. My process has been a testament to the faithfulness of God to point me toward home; my heavenly home, while traveling this earth.

God did not say the Christian life was free of pain, nor did He say that as a pastor I would not experience failure, but He did say He would cause me to triumph. The loss of my Vincent has taken me to a suffering place, and through the dark night of the soul. God, the author of my faith, has given me the ticket I needed to make it through victoriously. I am indeed different. I am more dependent. I am more vitally connected to the Vine. I am alive again. I feel great joy and great exuberance for having passed through my sorrow and great anguish.

When we have taken this journey to our suffering place; when life as we know it is taken from us; when we endure the dark night of the soul; when we emerge on the other side with our life given back to us, we will not waste it on anger, jealousy, envy and strife. We will embrace life in every form and respect the sanctity of it.

I continue to pastor, and I feel that I am a better woman for having found life to be so fragile, precious. I am better equipped and prepared for my calling. I am more tolerant of weakness in both myself and in others. I am thankful for each new day. I can say with assurance that my God is faithful.

I love the Lord. I love His church and His people with all of my being. I cannot wait until the train comes for me. I will have my ticket, and I will remember this place and that place, this mountain area and this valley. I will discover new things like a child on Christmas morning. I will wait excitedly for my King. I will kneel and worship at His feet, singing a song of adoration to celebrate my beloved. And then, having done all of these things, having been tried in this life so that I might be approved in the next, I will turn to see my son running to embrace me, and I will remember why I sing, "Oh Death, Where Is Thy Sting?"

I know the overtures of the Bridegroom. I know that death is a precious reunion. I know that I have been crushed so I may be purified.

I know my identity is gone so that His is increased. I know that strength comes from humility and intimacy. I know Jehovah Rophica, my Healer. I know Jehovah Jireh, my Provider. I know that satisfaction is greatest with patience. I know that earthly life is trivial in the face of eternity. I know that His vision is realized as I am perfected in the dark night. All of this I have learned on my journey to a place called 'there.'

Journal